SHOP TALK

SHOP TALK

POEMS FOR SHOPWORKERS

Tanner

PENNILESS PRESS PUBLICATIONS

Published by

Penniless Press Publications 2019

© Paul Tanner

The author asserts his moral right to be identified as the author of the work All rights reserved. No part of this publication may be reproduced, stored in a retrieval system or transmitted in any form or by any means, electronic, mechanical, photocopying, recording or otherwise, without the prior permission of the publishers ... lest we cut you, yeah? Too fucking right.

ISBN 978-1-913144-10-4

By the same author

Manifesto? (PPP)

The Ism Prison (PPP 2012)

Class Act (PPP 2015)

CONTENTS

REAL LIFE SOCIAL MEDIA	9
THE DEVOLUTION	11
GIVE A PLEB A NAME	12
WHAT YOU WANT	13
DEIGNED, LIKE	14
NO, SERIOUSLY	15
THE LUXURY OF BEING A VICTIM	17
4 TIMES	19
REVENGE ON THE PUBLISHED	20
BEAUTIFUL AND FECKLESS	22
TOMORROW'S BASTARDS TODAY	24
PRIORITIES	25
THEY SAYS	27
SHOPS ARE FOR SHOPPING	29
THE PROMISE OF A THREAT	31
?	32
I'VE WRITTEN THIS POEM BEFORE	33
I MISS THE STIGMA	35
BALANCE	37
THE FINE LINE BETWEEN BEING MISANTHROPIC AND SIMPLY BEING TIRED OF EVERYONE'S CRAP	39
THE CLOPEN	40
"I'M JUST GIVING YOU SOME FEEDBACK"	42
DO YOU NEED HELP?	43
MYSTERY SOLVED	45
THE HETROSEXUAL	46
VARIOUS DEGREES OF GARBAGE	47
JANUARY'S COCOON	49
LOST IN THE SUPERMARKET	50
HATE WORTHY	52
WRUNG NUMBER	53
1 QUESTION FOR EVERYONE	55

TIME, LINED	57
LIKE A PLATINUM CANCER	58
SEPARATE, DESPARATE	59
YAWN AWNING	60
IN DEFENCE OF SELF-SERVICE CHECKOUTS	61
PREPARED LIKE A MEAL	62
EVERYONE LOVES DEATH	63
ANOTHER LATE ONE	64
MY FINAL WEEK IN BIRKENHEAD	66
INKED … UP? DOWN? ON? NO … IN	68
LIKE IT'S A BAD THING	70
YOU'RE NOT WELCOME SO YOU'RE WELCOME	71
"OUR STAFF WILL NOT TOLERATE ABUSE"	73
JINGLE BELL END	75
I DON'T KNOW WHAT "MAN" MEANS ANYMORE	76
SUFFERING FOR YOUR FART	78
BIRKENHEAD REVISITED	80
THE UNBALANCED BALANCE OF THEM	83
UNREASONABLE REFUND POLICIES FOR UNREASONABLE REASONS	85
IN RESPONSE TO EVERY ARGUMENT THAT EVER HAPPENED IN ANY SHOP EVER	87
CONFESSION (OR: "WHY DON'T YOU EVER WRITE ABOUT TRUMP, ARE YOU A NAZI OR SOMETHING?")	88
HONEST TO DISHONEST GOD CONVERSATION I JUST HAD	91
THE CLOSEST THING TO REBELLION	93
EXAMPLES	95
THE TERRIBLE BURDEN (SHE WANTS TO SPEAK TO THE MANAGER)	96
CHOICES	99
THE GROUND BETWEEN US	101
THEY ALL	103
THE COMPETITIVE UNITY OF THE DAMNED	105

YOUR BOSS SMILES	108
ORIGINS UPON ORIGINS	109
SUPERS	111
JUST A SNIPPET OF THIS LIFE	117
INSPECTION	119
WOMEN'S FIB AND OTHERS	121
COLLECTIVE WHAT	123
LABELS LIKE BUMPER CARS	124
I'M LOWER THAN A NONCE IN THE FOODCHAIN	126
WE BURN	127
DRIVEN	128
NEVER SURPRISED, ALWAYS AFFECTED	129
THE (A) INTERVIEW	131
COMMEMORATING MY 1000TH COMPLAINT	133
THE SUPERIOR EDUCATION OF THE UNEDUCATED	134
O(ri)FFICE	135
CONTACT	137
THE PROTESTOR	138
GAS ATTACK	140
A SLIGHTLY BETTER CLASS OF SLAVE	141

REAL LIFE SOCIAL MEDIA

they moan about the greedy
and want discounts on everything,

they cry about waste
and dump meat to rot on shelves,

they mourn the environment
and litter everywhere,

they bemoan hierarchy
and want to see the manager,

they fret about unemployment
and try to get you fired,

they warn of the nanny state
and want you to wipe their arses for them,

they vent on the pressures of parenthood
and want you to wipe their kids' arses for them,

they express disbelief at the failure of the working class to unite
while teaching their children to fear or hate you,

they reel about modern life being too busy
and form queues,

they think Christmas is too commercialised
but they can barely go one day without shopping,

they say shops are taking over
and hang out in them all day,

they wax on about narcissism
and fly off the handle
at the tiniest thing
and/or nothing at all,

they campaign against bullying

but if they see you being abused,
verbally or physically
they either stand by
or join in,

they debate
the supposedly modern phenomenon
of snowflakes
and have always
always
demanded special treatment

everything
you think you know
about yourself
and everyone else?

go work in a shop.

THE DEVOLUTION

our unelected Lizzie's face
clamped between yellow NHS chompers,
our witty Whinnie's baby mush
coated in green spit
…
after getting the flu 3 times
I'd had enough,
so I got a piece of A4 paper, wrote
I WILL NOT ACCEPT MONEY
FROM YOUR MOUTH on it
and stuck it on my checkout station …

kid you not, I had 8 –
that's right, 8 –
customer complaints
until someone ran and got the manager …

I'm serving a society
that demands the right to infect me,
literally dripping benefit money from their orifices
onto those willing and able to work
until the infection takes hold.

it's hardly surprising
Darwin was taken off the tenner.

GIVE A PLEB A NAME

she said I just want to grab some bits,
I'll be really quick!
but I stood firm in the doorway:
I'm sorry, I said, but we're closed.

what's your name? she demanded.
paul, I pointed at my name badge. why?

she marched off ...

I lay thinking about it all night:
surely she won't try anything personal?
I mean, we were closed, so the worst she could do
is complain to head office about our opening hours, surely?
... so why did she want my name?

I go in the next day and the manager shows me the email:

one of your workers SLAMMED the door in my face!!
he said his name was "PAUL" but that was probably a LIE!?
are ALL of your workers so VIOLENT towards WOMEN??

she went on to say that she would never shop
in that store ever again ...
it's a shame "Paul" wasn't around to enjoy that.

WHAT YOU WANT

It must be bad, he says, working on boxing day?

I don't say anything. I carry on scanning his shit.

I'd hate it, he says, working in retail
at this time of year.

I don't say anything. I carry on scanning his shit.

Then again, he says, leaning in nice and close,
I suppose it must be bad any time of the year,
mustn't it?
and he smiles

so I give him what he wants:
I tell him:
only when I have to serve
bored cunts like you,

and his smile stays there
as he asks for the manager:

Merry Christmas, bored cunt.

DEIGNED, LIKE

it's not until
an editor rejects your poem
about two female customers
threatening you with a knife
on the grounds that
"it wasn't very believable"
that you realise most of them there
lefty men of literature
don't have a clue
about the working-class life
of retail

but you soon find yourself
begging for his forgiveness
and/or acceptance
like you beg
the very customers
you were writing about,
you lie and suggest they were rich and/or Tory,
you say it happened in a Waitrose
instead of Tesco Express,
for like the very customers
you were writing about,
he has the power
to censor you
with a knife
to your work and/or throat,
and fuck's sake, Mr Editor,
any writer will tell you
it's the same thing.

NO, SERIOUSLY

Four pounds fifty, I said.

HOW MUCH? he leaned over the counter.

Four pounds fifty, I said.

HOW MUCH? he cupped his ear.

FOUR POUNDS FIFTY! I bellowed.
he nodded, gave me the money.

Next please, I told the queue.

He was deaf, you know, said the next guy.

Yeah, I nodded. So?
and do you know what he said? he said:

So, that's no reason to YELL at him, is it?
No, seriously.
I thought he was making a bad joke,
so I automatically did what I always do
and let out a fake laugh.

OH, SO YOU THINK IT'S FUNNY, DO YOU? he flailed.
MIS-TREATING THE DISABLED?

so I asked him if he was aware
that he was now yelling at me,
and that having decent hearing
meant I was actually in
more pain than a deaf person.

HE DOES! he turned to the queue,
HE'S MAKING JOKES ABOUT DISABLITIES, HE IS!

long story short,
there's a disciplinary form somewhere
with my name on it

for, and I quote: "yelling at the deaf"
no, seriously.

my only hate crime
is that I hate
everyone equally, ok?

although some people
are more
equally
hateful
than others,

don't you find?

THE LUXURY OF BEING A VICTIM

I told them that will be twelve quid, please.

He held out a note.

I went to take it off him –

he pulled his hand back –

missed! he laughed.
his girlfriend laughed too.

you want it? he dangled it in front of me.

I reached for it again –

gotcha! he snatched it away again –
and ha ha ha, he laughed.

ha ha ha, his girlfriend echoed.

fine, I said. don't pay me.

eh? his face dropped.

walk out without paying, I said.
see what happens.

I was only messing, he said.

yeah, he was only messing! she said.

here, he held the note out, take it!

I took the note while she took the vodka bottles.

eight pound change, I held it out.

he reached for it –

I pulled my hand back –
missed! I laughed. ha ha ha!
you're right, it's fun, this game, innit?

they were so offended
that they made a complaint

which offended me,
but offence
is a luxury
I can't afford,
unlike
a grossly
overweight
unemployed
alcoholic
couple
who take the piss out of
minimum wage tax payers
then try to get them fired –

they're the real victims here.

4 TIMES

first was on the way into work,
she stopped me by the boarded up Threshers
and asked for 20p …

the second was when I was on my break,
was having a fag by the bins, thinking I was alone
but no – she practically jumped out of one,
asking for 20p again …

the third was actually in the shop,
she queued for 15 minutes
and when she got to the counter
she said, could I have 20p please
like she was asking to legitimately purchase
a lottery ticket or something …

now I'm about to go home
but she's out there,
I can see her waiting across the road …

doesn't she know about the rule of 3?
it's enough to make you go all Patrick Bateman on a bitch

except she's not homeless, despite how she looks
and she's certainly not a prostitute,
if said looks are anything to go by
and I don't work on Wall Street

in fact,
I don't even have 20p.

REVENGE ON THE PUBLISHED

you know jobs?
well I only went and got one:

my first shift
a customer poked my chest
and called me stupid

so I told them to back off
and they started yelling
that THEY
were being threatened
by ME

until my supervisor came running over,
apologised to the customer
on my behalf
and sent me to the manager's office,

where the manager tried
to get me to sign a piece of paper
saying I was in the wrong

so obviously I left,
went crawling back the job centre
where a job centre crony told me I was, quote,
a disappointment.

my passive aggressive customer? a woman
my supervisor? a woman
my boss? a woman
the job centre crony? a woman

and as I glance across this grey council room
where us scroungers sit circling jobs
in the free local papers,
my heart
and dick
sink
to see the men

outnumber the women
about 10 to 1
as it usually does on these jobseeker thingies.

could I be forgiven
for surrendering to
identity politics,
for thinking
everyone with a vagina
owes me an apology?

no
I'd be even more of a loser
than I already am

and so,
by the way,
is the oft published poet
who said I was
misogynist
for not liking
the Ghostbusters remake.

BEAUTIFUL AND FECKLESS

the customer said my stubble was off-putting.

the next time he saw me I'd shaved,
but he still wasn't happy:
broken out a bit, he said,
pointing at my spotty neck,
haven't you?

the next time he said my teeth were quite yellow.

time after that
he suggested I was quite below average height,
wasn't I?
and
at this point
I'd started to have enough, I mean,
if my appearance was so offensive to him
then why did he keep joining my queue?

so the next time he came in
and started telling me my hair was a bit loud,
or some other visual crime I was guilty of,
I asked him: does it work?

does what work? he asked me,
so I spelt it out for him:

does insulting a shop worker's appearance
make your dick any bigger?

given the amount of criticism he'd dished out,
I thought he could take this tiny scrap
of constructive banter,
that it might inspire him
to join another queue next time
and save himself the torture of having to look at me,
to move on with his life,
move on from me
and all my apparent warts and all

but I was dragged into the office,
where management told me
I "sexually molested with him" my words,
and I was lucky he wasn't suing,
I was lucky he only made a complaint,
that I was obviously hypersensitive
and not cut out for
dealing with people, and furthermore –

well, I don't know what more they said after that
because I walked out

where I joined the town centre rabble
doing their town centre rabble thing,
where no one singled me out
for my shoddy appearance
or nasty personality …

I had arrived:
I was finally
as beautiful and feckless
as the town centre rabble.

TOMORROW'S BASTARDS TODAY

The children trash the shop

the children throw things at the workers

the children blare porn full blast
from phones you can't afford

the parents just watch
or don't watch

they say things like
they get paid to clean it up
and don't tell my child what to do

and their children hear them
and their children learn from it:

they trash more of the shop,
they throw more things at the workers,
they blare harder and harder porn
louder and louder

and you look at them and you wonder:

why are they being taught to hate you?

are any of these
bloated insecure toddlers
with everything and nothing,
literally screaming out for attention
going to grow up
to be prime minister?

and the sad thing is
even you
don't know
if you're being sarcastic.

PRIORITIES

I was in aisle 7
mopping up a smashed jar of bolognaise
when he marched up to me:

got any Kitkats? he asked.

no, I told him, we've ran out.

I know! he nodded, I heard!

then why did he ask?

I couldn't believe me ears!
he stomped his feet,
I couldn't believe
ME FUCKIN EARS!

well … it's true, I said.
sorry.

NO, YOU'RE NOT!
he got closer,
BUT YOU WILL BE,
he lifted his jacket,
so I could see
the butt of his gun.

now
it was probably a toy
or a convincing pellet gun
maybe even a water pistol
but the point is:

he wanted me
to believe it was real,

he wanted me to believe
he was going to take my life

because the Kitkats had sold out –

not the customers that had bought them all,
not the company that hadn't ordered more,
but me:
a shopworker mopping up on aisle 7?

that's sad
and sadder still
is that he heard it on the grapevine:
pretty desperate grapevine this town has

but maybe the saddest thing of all
is that it wasn't a real gun
for I was always so sure
that I would have died how I lived:

mopping up on aisle 7.

now
not even the gods know
how the public will chose to end me,
or what aisle I'll be in …

THEY SAYS

she says
she doesn't need her receipt.

so I carry on serving
someone else
but then she comes back:

where's my receipt? she wants to know,
you didn't put it in my bag!

I tell her she didn't want it.

Are you telling ME what I want?
she flushes.
I think I know what I want better than YOU!

So I start routing through the bin for it ...

IS THIS GOING TO TAKE LONG?
she barks down at me,
as I'm on all fours,
picking through the rubbish.
I HAVE A PARKING TICKET, YOU KNOW!

EXCUSE ME! says my current customer.
YOU HAVEN'T FINISHED SERVING ME YET!

WHAT'S THE HOLD UP?
the next bloke in the queue says.
WHAT ARE YOU DOING DOWN THERE?

none of them talk to each other.

COME ON, MY TICKET IS GOING TO RUN OUT!
implores the bitch who wants the receipt.

YOU HAVEN'T FINISHED SERVING ME!
wails my current customer.

GET UP! THERE'S A QUEUE!
demands the bloke.
GET UP!

I'm amazing:
I'm an uneducated thirty-something
on minimum wage
who can't answer back,
outnumbered
on my hands and knees

and yet
I can still victimise
three people at once?

No wonder they're panicked.

SHOPS ARE FOR SHOPPING

if you don't like the price,
don't buy it.

if you don't like the bag charge,
bring your own bag.

if you parked on a double yellow,
move your car.

if you need sympathy,
see a shrink.

if you have a story to tell,
write it down.

if you want someone to laugh at your jokes,
go on stage.

if you want a fight,
take up boxing.

if you're in a rush,
if you have somewhere else to be,
or something else to do,
for the love of god,
don't go shopping

don't go shopping

don't go shopping
to satisfy any of these frustrations
or solve any of these problems

that's not shopping,
that's taking your shit life out
on someone who can't answer back

and finally
if you're concerned about unemployment

stop trying to get shopworkers disciplined
for not indulging you
in all of these frustrations and insecurities
under the vague umbrella term
of 'bad customer service'
ok?

because pretty soon
there'll only be those
self-service machines left
and we know how much
you all hate them:

after all,
you can't pass
your endless and varied
miseries
onto a robot,
can you?

THE PROMISE OF A THREAT

I must treat my wife
right
I must give her all of my
love
and I must give it all of the
time

I cannot be like the men
I serve in the shop:
divorced, unemployed, bitter children
lecturing me on how evil I am
for working for an evil company
that dares to charge them
for their ready meals and alcohol
with tax I earned

no

I cannot become one of them
can I? please Cheryl
know that I love you
with all of my love
all of the time

except when I hate
but not you, never you
how could I?

?

literally
everyone
I've ever served
seems to know
how to work in a shop
better than I:

seems like a waste of talent.
so why don't you work in a shop?
apparently
it's easy
apparently
they'll hire anyone
no matter how
lazy
or slow
or just plain stupid
apparently
you can even be ugly too

and the best part?
people
apparently smarter
and apparently better looking
than you
will "pay your wage"
for you to offend them
all day long

so ditch that tie
and pick up an application form today!

you don't need an education
but by Christ
you'll get one.

I'VE WRITTEN THIS POEM BEFORE

it's about this guy who lived in my bedsit,
horrible gummy-mouthed shit
claimed every benefit, he did
and he drank this nasty sugary rum,
and I knew that because I used to serve it to him,
in the shop around the corner,
he'd come in and I'd scan it through for him
and he'd leave without please or thank you
and I'd go home after my shift
and I'd find the bottles smashed on the stairs,
his vomit on the stairs,
vomit in the communal kitchen,
great orange lumps they were
and I'd have to clean it all up
before going to bed
and getting up and doing it all again
and after a while of this I got fed up,
so I wrote a poem
like the one that you're reading now
about it
about him
and what an ungrateful waste of life he was,
how his organs could've gone
to someone less gross and lazy and inconsiderate
if he hadn't pickled them already,
and would you believe
it got rejected?
the magazine said I was a snob:
picking on sick people unable to work, they said,
I'd obviously been manipulated by the right-wing media
and they couldn't
in good conscience
publish such divisive propaganda
and just to hammer home the point,
they didn't even send me the poem back,
they used the self-addressed stamped envelope I'd sent
to send the rejection slip back
and nothing else,
I guess it didn't occur to them

that this snob
didn't have the money to print copies,
and when I was done reading it
in the doorway of our bedsit,
I looked up to see him passed out on the stairs,
surrounded by bottle shards and vomit;
I had to kick him
to get him to move
and then, when he moved
I had to kick him again, cos, well, you know, just cos …

Anyway, second time's a charm,
and I think this poem
is better than the first one
so I ask the next esteemed editor:
will you reject it again?
and when you do,
will it be for confusing political reasons
or because it's simply not very good?

whatever the reason,
I can always go for a hat-trick
so actually,
reject it anyway:
you'll only give me
another poem

only
to write,
never to publish.

I MISS THE STIGMA

It used to be
you'd tell people you worked in a shop
and they'd get mad at you:

are you the manager?
no.

assistant manager?
no.

supervisor?
no –

I'm just a sales assistant,
you'd say apologetically

and when
in a state of disbelief
they'd practically beg you
to tell them
you were only doing this
to put yourself through college
and you gravely shook your head

they'd be so disappointed
in you
they'd leave finally you alone

which was great
because you had better things to do
than impress them

but these days
people are easily impressed:

they tell you how lucky you are
to have a job
any job at all
and then they leave you alone

which is a shame

because now
you are the supervisor
and the assistant manager
and the manager,
sometimes you're left with the shop keys for days,

it's just you're still paid
as a sales assistant

and you've still got
no higher education

and you want to talk about it
but you can't

because the sad thing is
you really are
comparatively
one of the lucky ones.

BALANCE

the one with shit stains
on the front of his tracksuit bottoms,
he wants to know
why your shop is closing down,
he's very upset by this,
upset enough to yell at you

you tell him you don't know,
you're worrying about rent,
you're wondering if
you've any friends left
who'll put you up,
you're wondering if
you've any friends left
full stop,
you're thinking maybe
being made redundant
will look bad
in future job interviews:
I'M REDUNDANT you hear yourself say
to a potential boss
and,
well, it doesn't sound good, does it?

and meanwhile shit dick here
is telling you how unhelpful you are:
no wonder you're closing down! he heckles …

you saw him down the job centre,
he was sitting on the steps
and he caught your eye,
and he asked you for money:

you told him to fuck off
his eyes widened

he stood up
presenting his shitty crotch,
he was about to say something –

but then he didn't:

you weren't at work now,
you could answer back now

and he turned away
so you could see
the piss stains on his arse ...

here you are
no more broke than when you worked,
with more rights and more respect
from the general public than you've ever had?

you could get used
to being redundant

in fact
you better had.

**THE FINE LINE BETWEEN BEING MISANTHROPIC
AND SIMPLY BEING TIRED OF EVERYONE'S CRAP**

"IS IT FREE?"
you must have heard that joke a thousand times
just this week,
every time a barcode didn't scan

you don't laugh?
the customer makes a complaint
you laugh?
the customer accuses you of patronising them
then complains

face it
you just aren't good
at navigating the minefield of human interaction
no matter how hard you try

so now you warn people
about being in your company:
after all
if you can't satisfy them
when your next meal is on the line,
how can you be expected
to perform for free?

THE CLOPEN

you stay behind after closing
while this lonely old prick
makes you escort him
up and down the aisles
asking you what you think
of everything in the shop:

what's these kidney beans like?
he wants to know.
you tell him you've never tried them
and he's outraged:
you're supposed to be a salesman!
he scolds you,
there's no passion
in customer service anymore!

it goes on like this
for quite some time,
time
that you are not getting paid for,
being harangued
from aisles 1 to 13,
from fruit to frozen

and when it's done
he makes you count out
eighteen-pound ninety-seven
in fucking silver ...

you finally lock the doors
behind you both
and as he shuffles towards his car
you run to the bus stop
but you've missed the last one
and you have to walk it:
he drives by you
on the flyover,
his brown Volvo
like a slow giant fly ...

you lie in bed, overtired
pretending to sleep
for like 3, maybe 4 hours?
then head back in

and Lonely Old Prick is there
at the shop doors
waiting:

he says you bullied him
into buying stuff he doesn't want,
he says
you gave him the hard sell,
he says
it's shameful, fleecing the elderly
and
there's no compassion
in customer service anymore!

and that's how
you became an advocate
for euthanasia

but it's not ageist:
you believe in
passionate compassion
for all customers
of all ages,
you tell yourself
as you sharpen the blade.

"I'M JUST GIVING YOU SOME FEEDBACK"

if my employers
listened to me
do you think
I would be here
serving you?

DO YOU NEED HELP?

no, she says,
I'm fine thank you,
I'm not stupid!
her necks wobble,
you think I don't know
how to shop by myself?

so I leave her and her chins
to it,
go back to stacking jars …

some other woman
comes up to me,
asks me to take her to the electrical section.

we're walking off and I hear:
HEY, WHERE ARE YOU GOING?

I turn
and it's the first woman,
waving her hairy bingo wings.

I NEED YOUR HELP NOW!
she ripples in panic.

I'm serving someone at the moment,
I tell her.

OH! she jiggles, SO
JUST BECAUSE I REJECTED
YOUR HELP BEFORE,
YOU'RE GETTING YOUR REVENGE NOW,
ARE YOU?

breathe.
count to ten.

I'll be back

when I've helped this lady,
I tell her. ok?

DON'T PATRONISE ME!
red waves ripple
her huge shapeless body.

well, I tried.

me and my new customer,
we walk away,
her yells echoing
down the aisle:

SOME PETTY PEOPLE
              WORKING HERE!
                          VERY PETTY!

as I reach behind me,
and I just happen to
scratch my back
with one solitary finger.

MYSTERY SOLVED

I wanna bring this back, he says
I can't refund this, I tell him.
yes you can! he says. you HAVE to!
it doesn't fit!
that may be, I explain,
but the blood stains on it
make it non-returnable.
they must have been on there
when I got it! he reckons.
no they weren't, I assure him.
I served you, remember?
you threatened me
when I wouldn't give you
a free bag?
well then how else
could they have got there, eh?
he asks. HOW ELSE?
as he reaches over the counter for me …

THE HETROSEXUAL

I'll be back! he vowed,
I'm gonna come back
with 10 or 20 men!
I know loads of lads!
don't think I don't,
cos I do!
and when a busy turned up
and asked him to leave
he wrestled him to the ground ...

it was all my fault:
when he told me
I looked like a faggot
as I bagged his groceries,
I had the gall to suggest
"well, you would know".

anyway, last I heard
he was, quote,
"inside"
but, question is:
who?

VARIOUS DEGREES OF GARBAGE

the boss,
he tells me to chuck out
all that old shelving.

that's metal, I tell him.
you need to ring recycling
to pick it up or something.

don't give me that hippy crap,
the boss has spoken.
just do it!

so I drag it all out
and I'm dumping it in the bins,
making this almighty clatter –
BUNG! BING! DUNK! –

during which
of fucking course
the fucking bin men turn up

one of them goes:
you're breaking the law,
dumping that shit!
you guys
need to arrange a recycling pickup!

I'm the only one here,
I tell him, looking around.

so? he says.

so "guys" is plural, I inform him.
didn't they teach you that
in bin man school?
he shoves me –
I go clattering into
the stacks of rubbish,
my landing

wet
yet
sharp,
splattered with stale coffee
but stabbed with shelf corners.
fuckin snob, he snorts
as they walk off …

I go tell the boss
the bin men wouldn't take our rubbish
and he starts yelling
but my mind is elsewhere:

what am I,
a hippy?
or a snob?

I suppose
in about 20 seconds
I'll be unemployed
and then I can be
whatever the hell I want

as the cold frappuccino
turns my blood brown
in an everyday open wound.

JANUARY'S COCOON

she's actually crying,
lying there clutching her stomach
shivering with anxiety

she has to go back to
her office job
tomorrow
and after 2 weeks off
she doesn't know
if she can take it

meanwhile
you've been working through
the whole of Christmas,
in fact
the worst is nearly over

and is that
the quiver of a smile
across your supermarket
air-con mummified lips
as you
look
down
at your social superior?

LOST IN THE SUPERMARKET

I was wheeling my cage of stock out
onto the shop floor
when he first approached me:

I built this! he declared. I built this building!

I just nodded
and carried on dragging my cage
through the general pubis:
excuse me, sorry, thank you, excuse me ...

I was putting tins out on the shelf
when he returned to me:
right where you're standing!
he bent over, pointing at the floor.
the ground beneath your feet
is literally thanks to me!
he said
and he stood there, waiting for thanks ...

I just nodded and carried on stacking tins ...

I was wheeling my cage of stock back
through the shop floor
when he found me again:
got laid off! he wailed.
built this place
with half the men
and half the resources
and what thanks do I get?
they laid me off!

I just nodded
and carried on dragging my cage
through the general pubis:
excuse me, sorry, thank you, excuse me ...

last time I saw him,
he was in the electrical section

looking around,
sweating.

where's the exit? he grabbed me.

where you built it, I told him.

his face contorted
as he wrestled the appropriate response
before finally
reluctantly
nodding,
resigned to the lie
and he wandered off …

good luck to him:
I've been trying to leave for years.

HATE WORTHY

despite the heinous hypocrisy
of our half-chosen leaders,
besides the odd meme
and Facebook petition,
people more or less leave them to it

but if you want to believe a shop worker
so much as looked at you funny,
you'll go out of your way
trying to get them fired?

maybe shopworkers and politicians
should swap wages
to justify these paradoxical standards:

that way
when you blame us
as tax funded entities
for everything,
you'll be that rarest of creatures:
a customer
who's actually right.

except all the times you're wrong,
obviously.

WRUNG NUMBER

the phone rang.

it was so annoying
I actually picked it up:

what time are you open till?
snapped the woman's voice.

I told her.

well that's not very good, is it?
she said. I work,
I can't shop till later!

I'm sorry, I told her, but rules are rules.

you're not sorry!
the line crackled with her squawk.
if you were really sorry,
you'd stay open later!

so I told her
in all sincerity:
I don't make those decisions.

yes, I know that! she said.

well … then why are you
telling me
to extend the opening hours?

well, because!
she said.
because, well,
I'm just saying!

I was getting bored now.

well if you've got time

to "just say"
I suggested,
then you've got time
to shop, haven't you?
and I hung up.

half an hour later
this woman marches up to me:

WHERE'S THE SMART ALEC
I SPOKE TO ON THE PHONE?

see, I said,
you did have time to come in,
didn't you?

she didn't see the funny side
but to be fair
there wasn't one.

1 QUESTION FOR EVERYONE

why
when I yell through the glass
that we're closed
do you look
at the opening hours sign
to see if I'm lying?

and while we're on the subject,
let me ask you another one:

why
didn't you look at the opening hours sign
in the first place?
it was right by your face!
in fact,
you had to duck under it
to look through the glass
and bang on the door!

actually, fuck it, I'm adding a third:

didn't the fact
that the door didn't open
when you tugged at the handle
tell you all you needed to know?

and since we're here,
let's make it four:

why,
having established
the door was locked,
did you proceed
to duck under the opening hours sign
and bang on the glass
until I had to come over
to tell you
we're closed

which started this ridiculous charade in the first place?

you breed
and you vote
and it scares me shitless

so please,
kill yourself
and donate everything
but your brain

and that time
I wasn't asking.

TIME, LINED

then?
a caveman
stands at the mouth of his cave,
looking over the hill, thinking:
they've either got better meat
over there
and they're not sharing it
or they've got no meat
over there
and they're coming for ours,
either way
let's spear them first!

now?
a townie pleb
looks at a shop worker, thinking:
they've got a job,
they probably think
they're better than me
or they hate their job
and will take it out on me,
either way,
let's make the first
passive aggressive move!

Good species, this,
rich history.

LIKE A PLATINUM CANCER

he said
you shouldn't charge these prices
I said
I don't decide the prices
he said
I know, I'm just giving you feedback
I said
but what can I do with that feedback
if I don't make any decisions?
he said
I know, I'm just saying,
you shouldn't charge these prices …
I said
I don't decide the prices
he said
I know, I'm just …

and it went on like that
for quite some time
15 years, in fact since I left school.
been quite the education
and it's not over yet.

they tell me
none of us are immortal
but working in retail
feels life-threateningly close to it.

SEPARATE, DESPARATE

I was close to tears I was so
angry and run-down
from a 12 hour shift at the shop,
I thought:
no one feels as low as I do right now,
this blood-draining hate,
this warring mix of wary and rage

but I passed a parked car
and there was a bloke sitting in it,
tie wonky across his sweaty shirt
just rubbing his eyes
with his clenched fists
rubbing his face
in his car
like he couldn't go
in his house

and seeing this I didn't feel any better
but I didn't feel any worse either
and yeah, they say misery loves company
but if he had asked me how I was
I'd have chinned him
and I dare say he'd have done the same:

empathy
from a safe distance, then,
like everything else.

YAWN AWNING

got threatened again today
yeah yeah, I know I should just man up,
but bigger balls or thicker skin
aren't a satisfactory alternative
to good old fashioned revenge

shame it didn't happen in a pub,
someone might have had my back,
or if it happened on the street
someone would have called the police
and if it happened on the internet
the narcs would be tearing down their front door:

all of which
would have given me a vengeful laugh

but I wasn't threatened
in a safe and civilised place
like a pub or an alley or the internet

no, sadly it was in a shop
and sadder still?
I work there
and therefore
I am not allowed revenge
hence this poem:

Adam Johnson of Birkenhead,
if I wasn't at work
I could have taken you,
and even you
aren't too stupid
to know it,
you fat pin dick.

IN DEFENCE OF SELF-SERVICE CHECKOUTS

he didn't smell of alcohol
he didn't have needle marks on his arms
he seemed like he had some money
in fact, he was quite well-put together
clean shaven and fresh smelling,
why, he looked normal,
I suppose you'd call it
so,
what if he is normal?
what if he has a job and a family
and what if he's halfway decent,
what if he's a doctor or a carer,
a regular donator to charities,
kind to animals and patient with children,
all of that, right,
but my subservient face
was just too tempting
and that's why
he had to throw those biscuits at me?

I think I'll just start saying
UNEXPECTED ITEM IN THE BAGGING AREA
whenever I'm approached, it'd be better for you
and me.

PREPARED LIKE A MEAL

every time,
every job you get
it's always the same:
they make you watch a health and safety video.

you already know how to pick stuff up,
you know not to drink bleach,
you know all about gravity
and that a messy shop means
you're more likely to trip
and meet the floor

but they never tell you
how to deal with the general public

how can they?
where would they begin?
if they tried to sum up
the physical and mental dangers
of being trapped on a floor
with that psycho crowd
you wouldn't even last
the training period

you'd run away
but you wouldn't get far,
you'd get as far
as the next job
in the next shop
watching the next training video
because
you know,
you need to eat
and stuff?

EVERYONE LOVES DEATH

I'M DYING, he said
DOESN'T THAT MEAN ANYTHING TO YOU?
he's been in the shop every day since
so whatever is killing him
is taking its sweet time,
but quite why he wants to spend
his long slow death in this shop he hates
is beyond me …

I NEED TO PAY FOR MY WIFE'S FUNERAL!
he told me,
but he wasn't wearing a ring
which suggested he was already over it …

MY SISTER DIED LAST YEAR, she said …
now that one that might have been true
but I think said dead sis
would have been miffed
to hear that her death
was only worth
a fiver off some clothes,
for that was the reason she brought it up
for you see:

all of these complaints were made
in an attempt to get a discount.

no wonder death is so popular:
it's cheap and everywhere
like those it kills.

ANOTHER LATE ONE

you do the math:

4 of us behind for an hour,
at minimum wage that's 8.21 x 4,
that's 32.84 quid a night,
she's running the show 5 nights a week,
so 5 x 32.84 is 164.20!
times that by 4,
that makes 656.80 a month!

that's mad, you could get another worker with that,
or 2 part timers,
so everything would get done,
and no one
would have to stay back!

you put this to your boss
and she says no

and you can't help but worry
that capitalism isn't about saving money,
it's about keeping the workers
few and far between
so they're too tired to fight back,
but you quench these conspiracy theories,
and you try a different angle, you suggest:

let's go home when we close,
tell head office everything's done,
you'll have saved them like 650 a month,
they'll be chuffed with you, and we get
some evening slither of our lives back,
happy days, yeah?

but she won't listen
and when you're teaching capitalists
how to be more capitalist
to no avail
something's gone wrong

with capitalism
and your life
and hers

actually, that's a point:
she's salary,
she gets paid the same
whether you all stay late or not

so you try a another approach, you ask her:
haven't you got a life outside of this place?
and when her response
is to fire you
well, the answer was obvious all along really
wasn't it
and now you can't afford one either

but then, you never could
so maybe you don't understand capitalism

or maybe you do
all too well.

MY FINAL WEEK IN BIRKENHEAD

she told me
her and her daughter
were going to wait outside the shop
after closing
and stab me

she even showed me the knife:
little blunt thing
tucked in her pink tracksuit bottoms,
strong handle,
you could tell it would hold up
under a good carving

and then they left
with a "tick tock cunt"
out of herpes dotted smiles …

It's my fault:
I wouldn't serve them
because I was going on my break
after an 8 hour shift,
I mean, the nerve

totally reasonable response
on their part really
and I looked forward
to their blunt little education

but alas,
they never kept their promise

and to this day
I think I see them,
I double-take
in the street
at the bus stop
but especially at the queues I serve:

every face of scabs

every girl in pink

shit
look at that one,
what's that on her lip?
oh
it's just the common cold sore
never mind

what? no
I wasn't scared
don't be silly
I'm a man
I don't know what that is
but I am one
no
these are tears of sorrow
that I missed out on
their cutlery-based wisdom

that's why
I'm still looking over
my big manly shoulder.

INKED ... UP? DOWN? ON? NO ... IN

I've been a table
for many:
bosses
delivery drivers
and customers,
they've all used my back
to sign forms
and crunch numbers

sometimes I turn for the mirror
and I think I see them:
all those corporate numbers
and company signatures
imprinted on my back,
overlapping hieroglyphs
of a working-class life
dotted like
bullets, like
spider bites
across my shoulder blades

once a boss
used my back
to sign his name
to my own disciplinary form
after bawling me out:
I think that one
is permanently imbedded
he pressed so hard,
a carver he was
and he had a big manager's desk
he could've done it on
but whatever
I can still see it
running down my spine
now

maybe I should get it
tattooed on me,

wouldn't that be cool,
wouldn't that be evidence
of my underdog rebellion?

wait
what
I want to stain my body
with a superior man's name
and parade it around
with something like pride?
typical
confused plebeian bravado,
that is,
no wonder
I'm working class
no wonder
I'm a table

next I'll be asking them
to cut off my ears
and make me fight
with literal underdogs
to make them
even more money
and make them feel
like even bigger men

best not give them any ideas.

LIKE IT'S A BAD THING

Every time I come here, she said,
The customer service is terrible!

And yet, I told her,
You still come in
which means you want it,
so what you're saying is
my bad customer service
is good customer service
and I thank you
for the positive feedback!

and as if she hadn't done enough for me,
she then went and made
an official complaint,
letting my employers know
how disappointed she was
which really just proved my point
all the more

but I think they missed it
because they let me go

oh well
you don't have to be a genius
to work
or shop
in a shop

and if you were
I doubt it would help

but neither I
nor my boss
nor my customer
would know.

YOU'RE NOT WELCOME SO YOU'RE WELCOME

and lo,
the same old useful criticism is offered:
if you hate your job,
why don't you just quit?

well, let's
forget about food
and rent
and consider this:

maybe I'm not the one with the problem?

I may be hungry
uneducated
and own nothing

but retail
is a way to scrape by
while paying taxes

so if I quit tomorrow
not only would I be
killing myself
but the problem would still remain:

it's called the general public

that mob
hates shops,
hates shopping
in shops,
and the people who work in them
yet they can't stop doing it,

so addicted are they
to that hatred
that closing for one day of the year
freaks them out,
they can't go one day

without doing something they hate
among people they hate,
they have to come in Boxing Day
extra early,
extra angry
to make up for it

that's fucked up
that's a problem
that's urgent
and everywhere
and needs addressing now

so don't you see
when I tell you
bored
lonely
insecure
passive aggressive
class cannibal
cowards
to fuck off
I'm only trying to help?

"OUR STAFF WILL NOT TOLERATE ABUSE"

I've never worked in a place
that had that sign up,
not in 15 fucking years of retail

because it IS my job to take abuse,
my job is exactly THAT

and truth is,
even if I sucked your little dick
or licked your wide cunt
you'll still moan
that I wasn't really into it

because you don't WANT
to be satisfied,
you WANT a punchbag

WE TOLERATE ABUSE

and if we didn't
most of you
would be charged and barred
from your local shops

insult someone
and you've committed a hate crime

threaten someone,
the police give you a warning

get physical, you're charged with assault

insult or threaten to get physical online
and you'll be named and shamed as a cyber bully

but do any of these things to a shopworker?
"oh well, that's retail for ya"

because WE TOLERATE ABUSE

and if we didn't
most people in this country
would be starving criminals
instead of starving criminals
who can abuse us

yes, I'm a snob
a snob
who barely scrapes by
on taxable minimum wage
by being abused all day,
funny kind of snob,
that

for I too
am a contrary fuckup
in this contrary fucked up country.

JINGLE BELL END

Bet you're looking forward to some time off,
aren't you? Red Jimbob asked me
as I scanned his stuff.
(Red Jimbob doesn't work.)
Nope, I told him,
I'll be working Boxing Day.
You're open Boxing Day? he asked,
his face falling.
(Red Jimbob spends a lot of money here.)
Well,
I bagged his stuff up.
Yeah?
 Great, he sighed.
Now I'll have to come in, won't I?
(Red Jimbob comes in every day.)
Well you don't have to,
I suggested,
taking his money off him.
You could just stay at home,
and then I could too?
Oh, well that's gratitude for you,
isn't it?
Red Jimbob snatched his change,
snatched his bag of stuff
and off he went,
muttering …
(Red Jimbob obviously prides himself
on redistributing the wealth he claims,
but 8 cans of Skol a day
is a high price to pay
for keeping a minimum wage worker
paying taxes,
and I say
we should cut out
the half-cut middle man.)

I DON'T KNOW WHAT "MAN" MEANS ANYMORE

he waited
until he'd paid for everything
and taken his receipt
to say:

give us a bag mate.

OK, I said, that'll be 5p.

he said, just give us it.

I said oh yeah,
I'll take it out me wages,
shall I?

so? he said, it's only 5p.

why's it ONLY 5p
when it's MY money?

5p to every customer
in a busy shop
soon adds up

so I asked him
if he had any idea
how many pricks like him
I have to serve a day

and evidently
he didn't
because then he wanted
a big argument:

little pricks
with big arguments,
they're not unique

but congratulations, sir:
the size
and volume
of your argument
suggests you must be
one of the smallest pricks
I've ever dealt with.

SUFFERING FOR YOUR FART

first there was the smell

then, he came in shitting – no, really
he was doing a shit
as he hobbled into the shop,
his face was red and clenched
and he was groaning
as he came over to the counter,
and he was eating,
he was eating as he was shitting,
a big bar of caramel and chocolate,
the caramel a golden dripping tube
hanging out
of his chomping teeth
as he chewed
as he shit,
groaning as he chewed
and chomped all that brown and gold
around in his red clenched face,

the smell
was deafening

and he looked me in eye as he shit,
shivering and groaning against the counter
he looked me in the eye
and smiled through gritted
brown and golden teeth,
his tiny eyes
although tiny
and watering
still managed to find mine
and our eyes were locked
as his hairy brown eye cried brown and gold
like a second mouth
and when he was done
he hobbled back out …

but the smell stayed,

it was first one in
and last one out
… besides me, of course

what IS it about a shopworker
that encourages public defecation?
why did he choose me
to shit with?
did I look like I'd appreciate it?

then again
thanks for the material, perv

and thank you to my boss
who wouldn't let me go home
despite how scarred and nauseated I was
but instead made me get the mop –

it bought me a few extras lines to write
but
at what
cost?

more than minimum wage, mate,
I'm telling you.

BIRKENHEAD REVISITED

it was very simple: there were no jobs

people worked
in the same place
forever
or not at all

the job centre would demand
you apply for jobs across the Mersey
and not just in Liverpool city centre
but way out,
like in Toxteth, or even Southport
which is practically Lancashire

all that time and money
that could go on rent and food
spent travelling to an interview
you knew you wouldn't get:
it would go to someone local to them
who could cover at a moment's notice
not you:
a "plastic scouser"
a "woolly back" from Cheshire
who was being made to do it

the job centre knew it too
but they still threatened to cut you off
if you didn't go
for they had quotas to fill:
either get them a job
or cut them off

and there just weren't any jobs
anywhere nearby
anytime soon
and that's all there was to it.

In a fit of neo-libertarianism, or something,
maybe desperation?

I thought, what this town needs
is a big fuck-off ASDA,
just pave over half of it
and put a huge supermarket on it,
that'll make taxpayers and spenders
of all us locals …

many jobs
many places
many years later
I passed through that town
and they had done just that:

an ASDA was at the centre of everything
with everything else
kind of backing off from it,
every home and road
circling it in something like fear,
to the birds
it must have looked like
brick spiders
swirling down
the corporate plug hole,
it must have looked like that
to the sick grey birds above

and I asked an old mate:
did it sort the town out?
he said many lost their jobs
when the ASDA paved over the old shops,
but then most of them went to work in the ASDA,
so it was about the same,
same number of people working,
same not, really.

I don't know if it's better or worse
cos it's not even that different

so if you fear the march of progress,
don't worry:
nothing really changes

except the colour of your work polo
and of course
you age,
you're always aging
and shrinking

the only thing
that grows with age
is the progress
we leave
for our
shrinking
aging
children.

THE UNBALANCED BALANCE OF THEM

I wouldn't
I couldn't
reduce the price for him
and he said
YOU'RE WASTING MY TIME
AND YOU'RE WASTING YOUR TIME

so I told him
actually, I'm paid hourly

to which he responded
YOUR ATTITUDE IS ALL WRONG

and he was right
my attitude was wrong
in fact
I didn't even have one
and I was supposed to,
wasn't I? I was supposed to
share his misery,
go home and make bad decisions,
drink
and neglect my wife

but instead
I did my shift
and went home
and hugged my wife
and stayed sober
and read
and wrote

I balanced
work and life

while he
did neither

retired or unemployable,

with all the time in the world,
he spent it
accusing shop workers
of wasting his time

I think he's dead now
but let's be honest
he was already

and all he left behind
was a complaint
about my "bad customer service"

you see
you can either be
a good person
or a good worker –
you can't be both

and that is why
the good
can be as unemployable
as the bad.

UNREASONABLE REFUND POLICIES FOR UNREASONABLE REASONS

"I'd like to return this DVD, please."
"Ok."
"I've got the receipt!" she waves it in my face. "Look, it's here! Look!"
"Yeah, ok," I take it out of her shaking hand.
Why's she so pent up? I haven't refused her yet. I'm about to though…
"I'm afraid you've had this three months."
"Yeah? So?" she fires back. She doesn't seem surprised.
"Well, we can only do refunds within a week of purchase."
"But I didn't watch it!"
"You've had it for three months though …"
"I've been busy! I've got a lot going on right now!
My mother's been ill! I had to move house …"
"Wow," I rub my temple. "I'm sorry to hear all that, but –"
"No you're not!"
"What?"
"You're not sorry at all, so don't say you are,
when you're not, it's really patronising!"
Believe me, I want to reassure her,
I am genuinely sorry I'm talking to you.
But I bite my lip …
"If you were sorry, you'd help!"
she's leaning over the counter now.
"Telling me there's nothing you can do isn't very helpful, is it?
"Well …" I blink in the cloud of her dog breath.
"Would you rather I LIED, and said I can give you a refund,
when I CAN'T?"
"EX-KEE-OOZE ME?"
"Well …" I feel my face go red.
I wasn't trying to be funny.
Really, I just didn't know how else to answer the stupid question.
And it's not like I can ignore her.
I have to respond to everything she says
and I'm beginning to think she knows
that.
"Exactly!" she's smiling.

"Don't have an answer for that, DO you?" S
she sounds angry, but her face is smiling.
"Because you KNOW you're in the wrong!"
Seriously, why is she smiling?
"I'm in the wrong?"
"Yes! I want to speak to your manager!"
Great.
I've already called him over twice this morning,
at the request of such idiots.
If I do it again,
he's going to bollock me
for not being able handle customers on my own.
Or cut down my hours.
And I really want to keep this job, don't I?
"Miss, please," I beg of her.
"He'll tell you the same thing,
he doesn't decide company policy either."
"Not about that, about YOU!" she points at me.
"Me?"
"Yes! You're being VERY RUDE to me!"
And BOOM – suddenly it's about me
as a person:

just as it dawned on her
that pushing me around
wouldn't get her a refund,
she conveniently realised
that she was offended by me
on a personal level

but since she wants to make it personal:
did trying to get me fired
make your divorce any less painful
or was the tan line on your ring finger
always there?

IN RESPONSE TO EVERY ARGUMENT
THAT EVER HAPPENED
IN ANY SHOP
EVER

if you put
half as much energy
into attacking and threatening
shareholders
as you do
the people
who work in their shops,
you might get somewhere.

CONFESSION
(OR: "WHY DON'T YOU EVER WRITE ABOUT TRUMP,
ARE YOU A NAZI OR SOMETHING?")

the American president doesn't come into the shop
2 minutes before closing to pick a fight,

the American president has never threatened me
because I couldn't refund him,

the American president doesn't call me a sell-out
for charging him 5p for a bag

the American president
has never told me
how slow or stupid I am
or the ways in which I am ugly
then try to get ME fired
for bullying HIM

but my neighbours do,
my own supposed class brethren does

they treat me
the way the American president
apparently treats you,
their persecution
and god complex
costing me jobs,
driving me out

and I didn't even vote for them

of course I'm not a fan
of the American president,
I despise everyone in power
but that's not taboo,
I'm allowed to say
that

what is taboo
is to point out
that the most powerful people
in my life
are the general public,
that every customer
is my president

wherever I am,
anyone local
can walk in off the street
to take their bad day,
their bad life,
their power-mad insecurities
out on me

that's what it means
to be working class in this country:
to leave school
and go straight into retail
is to be cannibalised
by your own

the American president
has had less of a negative impact
on my life
than the general public

they
are my Trump

in fact
they're worse,
there, I said it:
they're worse
because they DON'T discriminate:
they don't care
if I'm black
or white
or born here
or not,

if they see me wearing that name badge
behind the counter
then I'm the enemy,
an enemy who can't answer back,
a convenient scapegoat you might say

and I will respond to my Trump
as you do yours:
I will look down on
the general public
for their insecure power trips
and poke fun
at their hair
their skin
their voice
and their body shape
and tell myself
it's satire,
whatever that is.

so you see
I'm always writing about MY Trump
just like you are yours

and until the day the comes
when I can end their presidency
by booting them out of the shop
for their
hypocritical
divisive
greed?

I always will.

HONEST TO DISHONEST GOD CONVERSATION
I JUST HAD

*It has oft been said
that when the gods wish to punish us, they answer our prayers;
on this Sunday morning I prayed for the bus to be on time
and as the gods saw fit to grant me a such a bus,
I was met at the shop doors by this woman:*

finally! are you opening now?

no. it's Sunday.

so??

so we open at half 10.

oh, for god's sake! well, when's that??

when's half 10?

yes?!

… well, when the little hand's on 10, and the big hand –

don't you patronise me!!

you asked me when half 10 would be –

yes, but there's no need to be so, well,
obnoxious about it, is there??

how else could I have possibly answered such a ques –

you haven't even opened yet
and already I've had bad customer service!!

probably because we haven't opened yet.

that's no excuse!!

it is literally THE perfect excuse.
we haven't opened yet
and already I've got a bad customer,
how'd you think I feel?

but, but –

but what?

but you're representing the company!!

and you're representing yourself.
who do I complain to?

your manager's coming!
look, your manager's coming,
and I'll be telling him all about this!!

about what?
about how you started an argument with someone
who dared to argue back?

but you work here!!

not at the moment I don't.

well by the time I'm done,
you won't be working here at all!!

*Quite what the gods were punishing me for I don't know,
but rest assured I'll never be early again;
in fact, maybe I won't go in at all.*

THE CLOSEST THING TO REBELLION

there was a while there
for a few years
where I'd only work at Christmas:

I'd spend all year drunk,
job hunting,
arguing and haggling
with job centre cronies

but around October, November
some shop would always take me on
as a Christmas temp:

ironically
it was the one time of year
I was guaranteed to be sober
and working,
while everyone else
was getting wasted
and calling in sick
I was covering their shifts:
doing their late shifts,
doing back to back shifts,
haggling and arguing
with a drunk workshy public
until the new year,
maybe the end of January
when it all calmed down a bit
and they'd say
ok, see ya

and back to the bottle I went,
back to the job centre I went,
to haggle and argue
with a council crony
until October, November
when another shop would take me on,
"only temporarily, mind …"
and I'd spend another festive season

in hell
...

when I finally
got sober
and started working all year round
I realised
I was never rebelling:

everyone
is always
drunk,
workshy,
haggling
and arguing,
maybe even more
than I ever did

now
as a sober worker
I really am rebelling
or at least
I'm as close to rebellion
as I can get:
the closest thing
I have to rebellion
is taking their shit
all year round

it may be the closest
any of us
will ever get.

EXAMPLES

I got a job
but it was killing me

so I went the job centre
but they were no help:
we're here to help the unemployed
they said, we don't fulfil our quotas
helping you

fine, I thought
so I quit my shit job
but then
when I went back
they still acted annoyed,
maybe even more so:
you quit your job? they said
we're not allowed to help you

what a useless job, I thought
no wonder they're always so angry

and they can't even quit
because they know if they did
the only people who could help them
were themselves
and certainly not
their replacements

a shit advert
for long-term employment
in a shit job,
despite their best
or worst efforts
they were certainly
leading by example.

THE TERRIBLE BURDEN
(SHE WANTS TO SPEAK TO THE MANAGER)

there's no way
she declares,
that your refund policy is right!
she's red and waving her fist,
spitting down her avalanche of necks,
she wants to speak to the manager,
she wants him
here
and she wants him
now

so you go get him
and he's annoyed:
handling the public?
this is beneath him, this is

he goes over
and they talk
no, they chat:
it's very polite
she's fawning all over him
nodding for no reason, nodding
and her jowls are wings taking flight,
laughing for no reason
saying I understand, I understand
and then she leaves, smiling ...

she seemed perfectly reasonable,
the boss says,
why couldn't you handle her yourself?

you try to tell him
she was different with him,
that she obviously just wanted
to be acknowledged
by someone with more authority

even though

you find his authority
very
local
in the grand scheme of things
but whatever
she's of that generation
that gets a wide-on
for managers and doctors and any other
supposed men
of any other
supposed authority

but:
no, he says,
I'm obviously better with people,
and if you don't learn how to
deal with people
you'll have a short history here,
I'll tell you that

people:
they're beneath him
and above you,
but he's good with them
and you're not

so
in order to maximise both our strengths
you say, you know,
and make the store run more efficiently,
why don't you stay on the floor
and I'll hide in the office all day?

you don't even want his wage,
you just want his pathetic local authority
but turns out
that authority
is just big enough
to have the luxury
of being offended,
same as the customer

and as you're walking across the car park
you see her routing through her bag for her car keys:
she looks up:

you give her the finger

she gasps,
those necks going like a raped accordion
and she scurries back into the shop
to make a complaint
about someone who
no longer works there

it must be nice
to be allowed to complain
not just on the page
like I am now
but in real life
with real life consequences
for those you complain about,
it must be nice
or is it?

ever noticed how all these people
more important than you,
all these customers and managers,
they always have more to complain about
than you?

their authority must be a terrible burden

funny that, innit
anyway, let's head down the job centre:
I'm sure you can find someone
with authority
to offend
there, too.

CHOICES

she wants a refund.

I can't give her one.

she says it's pathetic:
you're a bitter little man, she says,
because you only work in a shop.

even though
I still can't give her a refund,
I concede that I am indeed bitter.
happy now?

but it's not enough:
she says
she's going to sue.

I tell her, good luck,
the company is pretty big
and has armies of lawyers.

not the company, she says,
you,
I'm going to sue you.

I ask her why?
I clearly have no money
otherwise I wouldn't be serving you,
would I?

because the company
wouldn't get away with it
she says,
if people like you
didn't do its dirty work
for them.

she's gone from
snob

to victim
in about 8 seconds

I've gone from
pathetic
to powerful
in less

get me a neck brace
I'll sue this bitch
for political and social whiplash

since the company
certainly won't insure me
for such a thing
or anything else

as the bitch
bares her teeth

and the doors,
unobstructed by security guards,
let in the next customer
and they're carrying
one of our bags:

that'll be another refund.

THE GROUND BETWEEN US

"You CAN do me a discount,"
he points a finger.
"I KNOW you can!"
No, I can't.
"You're LYING!"
he slams his fist on the counter.
"You're LYING to me!"
I'm not.
"Well you would say that,
wouldn't you?"
he kicks the counter,
"You WOULD say that!
You think I'm stupid?"
There's no other staff around,
only customers
waiting for their turn
so I get up
and walk away …
"Where you going?"
he follows me across the shop floor.
"Running away are you?
Because I'm right,
and you KNOW I'm right!"
I go through the door
that says STAFF ONLY.
I go into the staffroom.
The supervisors jump
out of their chairs
in horror,
they drop their tea and biscuits
as they cry:
who's on the shop floor?
I grab my coat off the peg
and head back out …
My customer has been waiting for me:
"Going, are you?
Been FIRED, have you?
Not surprised!
When you LIE

to LOYAL CUSTOMERS!"
we're heading towards the exit …
"Like LYING to LOYAL CUSTOMERS,
do you? Like withholding discounts
from LOYAL CUSTOMERS?"
The automatic doors slide open …
"Make you feel like the BIG MAN, does it?"
I step outside
and he follows …
"Just because you JUST work in a SHOP,
you like taking it out
on the VERY people who pay YOUR wage,
DO YOU?"
I take a deep breath
and turn to him:
I just quit, I tell him.
We're outside.
You're yelling,
in the street,
at someone
who can answer back.
Do you understand
where I'm going with this?
and he
looks me up and down
with a practiced sneer
and he says
"Coward!"
before spitting on the ground between us
and marching off.

THEY ALL

think they're next

they all
want to push to the front of the queue

they all
think they're the only person in the queue

they don't know
they're pushing in
they don't know
they're in a queue
they don't know
I'm serving someone else

they only see me
and my badge

it's a target
that narrows their vision
until they can't see
won't see
anything
or anyone else
but me

and they just can't understand
why I'm taking so long
to get to them

they must think
I'm talking to myself
here, at my checkout station
while one of them,
another customer,
a customer here first,
chews my ear off
totally invisible
to the rest of them

so I take the badge off,
I remove the target
and I evaporate like a ninja

I walk through the shop
invisible
I leave the shop unnoticed

is this what it's like to be you lot?
no wonder you all cry for attention

my options are:
    1)   don't exist
    2)   exist enough to blame

as our superiors
rape the earth
they rent out to us
we get the governments
we deserve
as we queue up to make queues to queue up in

as we pretend we are superior
as we pretend we are all that matters,
but if no one else exists
then who or what
are we superior to?

exactly.

THE COMPETITIVE UNITY OF THE DAMNED

there's always someone
worse off

for every shop worker
that has been threatened
there's always another
that was actually attacked
for every shop worker
that was abused
there's always another
that went suicidal

we're as competitive
in our persecution
as the general public
that persecute us
for persecuting them,
it's true,

but nonetheless
it's truly true:

you think we exaggerate
the rabid insecurity
of the general public?

then congratulations:
there's someone
worse off than you

pity you're too ignorant
to ever know it

to be that ignorant
you must either be
educated
or a customer

and sometimes

somehow
you're both:

your education
never taught you
manners
and
your time at the job centre
never taught you
empathy

so consider this,
all of you:

for every shop worker
that takes your abuse
there may be another
willing to answer back:
sure
they'll be fired
maybe never get
another job again,
but you'll be in
tears
for the rest of your days,
maybe even take
your fantastic life
over the cruel words
thrown back at you
and let's face it:
if your insecurity
is so rabid
you have to abuse
a shopworker
you
probably
will

and for every shopworker
that is attacked
there may just be another

willing to hit back:
sure
they may be sued
or even imprisoned,
but what will you care
if they hit hard enough
to give you a brain bleed
or put their thumbs
in your eyes,
you'll still be
blind and dead
won't you?

let's face it: you always were.

YOUR BOSS SMILES

next week's rota is up:
your hours have gone down

you thought you saw your boss smiling today

maybe he cares about you as an artist?
he wants you to have
more time to write

so you go home
and you write a poem about it
see, it's working already

but then
the landlord comes knocking
you write about that too
but the ending's a bad one,
it's about someone
who gets thrown out on their arse

so you go begging your boss for your hours back

and your boss just smiles

you want to write about that smile,
but when?

you have to pay for an artistic licence
and by the time you've earned it
you can't afford it

either way
your boss smiles
but only with his mouth

and does he smile at home?
does your landlord?
do you?

ORIGINS UPON ORIGINS

hatred
is never returned
to its source

your man beats you
because his penis is too small

the customer wants you fired
because her man left her

the politician starves you
because daddy never hugged them

aye
hatred
it never comes full circle

it's broken up
and scattered,
each bit
of hate
gathers other
bits of hate
and they mix,
whisked by
us twats,
until we wouldn't recognise
our own hatred
being thrown back at us

that's it's power, mate
that's our weakness, mate

maybe that mad old bitch
rammed her shopping trolley
into the back of your knees
because she misses her late husband

so instead of bottling up your rage

and snapping at your girlfriend,
tell that mad old bitch:
even in hell
your husband isn't missing you

do it for a better world.

SUPERS

they'd keep you behind, unpaid
for 15 minutes a night
just because they could,
even if the shop was fully stocked and cleaned
they'd say WE'RE NOT BREAKING THE LAW
WE CAN KEEP YOU BEHIND FOR FIFTEEN MINUTES
WITHOUT PAY
and you'd have to stand there
on the clean fully stocked floor with them
for a quarter of an hour
after every shift,
their arms folded
staring at you:
an hour and a half of your life
robbed
every week

now and then
they'd call you up
to their little office of power
that hovered above the shop floor
and they'd ask:
TELL US SOMETHING YOU DON'T LIKE ABOUT US
and watch you squirm,
COME ON, they'd demand, THERE MUST BE SOMETHING
and you'd have to pick something
as trivial and non-personal as you could, like:
ok, you two do leave the staff room a bit messy,
which was an understatement
but you said it with a shrug
hoping you'd got away with it
and for weeks afterwards
they'd come into the staff room
when you were on a break,
yelling OH, SORRY I LEFT MY BAG ON THIS CHAIR
THAT PROBABLY ANNOYS YOU, DOESN'T IT?
and YEAH, AND SORRY I LEFT MY PHONE CHARGING
ON THE TABLE, BET YOU'RE MAD AT ME, AREN'T
YOU?

and they'd take sick days
saying you gave them O.C.D.
both of them
they'd take turns
taking sick days
citing THE STRESS CAUSED by you, and
YOUR CONSTANT CRITICISM

and remember when
one of them pushed you
and you fell over those boxes
and the other
said it was you
who pushed her?
I SAW THE WHOLE THING she said,
shame it happened in the warehouse
in that corner where there was no CCTV
but I SAW YOU PUSH HER
and they believed it,
fuck, when they said
YOU'RE LUCKY WE DON'T SUE YOU
you could see in their eyes
that they believed themselves
and one of them smacked your head
and the other laughed
and said IF YOU TELL, WE'LL TELL
and it was 2 against 1
and women to boot
so you just had to take it?
yeah, you remember

and just when it looked like
you were about to get
fired and/or arrested

… they fell out …

and you watched them cannibalise,
accusing each other
attacking one another

they started taking you aside
to recruit you:
IT WAS ALL HER FAULT one would say,
SHE TURNED ME AGAINST YOU, BECAUSE SHE HATES
YOU
and then the other would say SHE PROBABLY FANCIES
YOU
AND WAS JEALOUS OF OUR WORKING FRIENDSHIP
you know, both
getting more and more desperate
to fuck the other over
with your help

they'd make complaints to head office
on your behalf:
SHE BULLIES HIM one would say
SHE KEEPS HIM BEHIND EVERY NIGHT the other would
say,
SHE'S BEEN AGGRESSIVE TOWARDS HIM
followed by SHE'S BEEN SEXUALLY AGGRESSIVE
TOWARDS HIM
on and on
and somehow it was worse
than their joint attacks,
because now you were being recruited
on both sides
like working there at all
wasn't enough of a submission,
now you had to dodge the bullets
of two personality cults, weave
the shots –
and when someone from head office came to investigate
you always ended up
looking like the trouble maker anyway,
because even the complaints they made
about each other
were about you,
your personality
your feelings
were the issue,
not theirs,

jesus, even the manager
who spent his time between several stores,
he stayed for longer than 10 minutes one time,
just to have a meeting with you personally, just
to say: maybe you're too sensitive for retail?
which was true
but not the issue,
let's be honest,
you still don't know
what the issue was
because the issue
was theirs, not yours
but anyway, he said the paperwork
of all these grievances
was killing him,
and you were lucky
you had 2 supervisors
who kept going out of their way
to accommodate you
and your needs and feelings, but come on,
just get on with it,
if you've got a problem with them
maybe YOU should
just go

but head office didn't see
how they were to each other
when they weren't "saving" you:
YOU'RE FAT one would say
SPOTTY BITCH the other would retort
YOU'VE GOT HERPES the first would venture
YOU WISH YOU HAD HERPES the second responded
YOU FAT SPOTTY BITCH VIRGIN
when they weren't eating each other's Ryvita
or sending lewd texts to family members
on each other's phones

it was getting too much
they were going too far

and then
just when they seemed destined
for mutual destruction

… they made up …

and guess what?
they weren't happy
about how you'd been
shit-stirring between them,
oh no, HOW DARE YOU COME BETWEEN THEM?
YOU clearly had some DIVIDE AND CONQUER thing
going on, you did,
you CHILD
you SAD LITTLE MAN
why didn't you GET YOUR OWN LIFE
instead of MEDDLING IN OTHER PEOPLE'S BUSINESS
you know, because their lives
were so important to the universe,
so rich and satisfying
that you couldn't help but be jealous of them?
and you had to go back
to the unpaid 15 minutes
after each shift,
the meetings
where they dared you to insult them
the breaks
where they'd follow you around,
telling you you were victimising them
amid the warnings
always the warnings:
you'd BETTER BE CAREFUL
because YOU'LL GET WHAT YOU DESERVE ONE DAY

in the end
you did,
in the end
it was simple:

you got so drunk one night
you woke up

on the other side of town
and never made it back again.

forgive the anti-climax,
but such is life

and it's funny
how much you were drinking
at the time,
wasn't it?

do you ever think about them?
just think

they'll be someone else's boss now
maybe someone's wife
my god, even someone's mother
yep, they'll be breeders all right
how can they not be?
such lineage
can only thrive
in this world

I bet they have
thousands of followers
on some social media thing,
their narcissistic dramas
reaching further
than your literary efforts

because you do write
don't you,
you write
and you still think about them

but you're not bitter, are you?

and by you
I mean me
don't I?
you tell me.

JUST A SNIPPET OF THIS LIFE

I WANT TO RETURN THIS.
ok.
I DON'T WANT IT, I WANT A REFUND.
ok.
I WANT A REFUND AND I'M ENTITLED TO ONE.
yeah, ok, can I just see your receipt?
I'M WELL WITHIN THE TIME LIMIT FOR A REFUND!
yeah, I just need to see the receipt.
WELL, IF YOU'RE GOING TO ACCUSE ME OF LYING …
I'm not, but obviously I need to see –
THERE! THERE'S MY RECEIPT! HAPPY NOW?
yeah. great. thanks. I just need to see –
WHEN I BOUGHT IT? IT'S THERE! LOOK!
THERE'S THE DATE, RIGHT AT THE TOP!
yes, I'm familiar with how our receipts look, thank you.
WELL THEN WHY DO YOU NEED ME TO SHOW YOU?
I didn't ask you to show me, I asked to see it because –
BECAUSE YOU THOUGHT I WAS LYING?
no –
WELL IF YOU'LL LOOK AT THE DATE, YOU'LL SEE
I WASN'T LYING, WAS I?
no, I know –
SEE? I TOLD YOU I BOUGHT IT
WITHIN THE TIME LIMIT!
yes, ok.
BELIEVE ME NOW, DON'T YOU?
I did anyway, I just needed to see –
YOU JUST NEEDED TO SEE IF I WAS LYING, DID YOU?
well … you know what? yeah. yeah, I did.
I KNEW IT! I KNEW YOU'D THINK THAT!
and obviously you know I need your receipt …
HE ADMITS IT! HE ADMITS TO CALLING ME A LIAR!
… otherwise you wouldn't have brought it in, would you?
IS THAT ANY WAY TO TREAT A CUSTOMER?
so why are you so offended by me taking said receipt?
SOMEONE WHO PAYS YOUR WAGE?
actually, that question was rhetorical.
JUST BECAUSE YOU HATE YOUR JOB?
because I know why.

IF YOU HATE YOUR JOB THAT MUCH …
and since you're obviously so determined to see my head roll,
I might as well earn my complaint and say why, anyway …
… YOU SHOULD JUST QUIT!
… mightn't I, you bored lonely fat bitch cunt?
AFTER ALL, IT'S NOT MY FAULT, IS IT?

whereupon:
walk outside, punch a lamppost,
mutter something about "class cannibals" and hate
everyone/thing,
but especially how normal you are being,
head in whatever direction,
towards whatever,
just sucking your knuckles –
knuckle sucking in aimless rage in town,
it's just too normal,
isn't it just?
and yeah.

INSPECTION

you mop up
sick and piss

you brush up
pastry and soil

you pick up
finger nails and snot balls

you scrape
half-digested crisps
and jellified spit
up off the floor

you leave the place spotless
then
go back to your rented room,
witness the mould dripping black
into the soggy skirting boards.

the point,
the irony,
the unfairness
of the situation
is obvious
but still,
there must be a more poetic line
to end on?
no
I can't think of one.

anyway
the next morning
the inspector from head office
finds a fat fuzzy dead moth
in aisle 6 – that's condiments and sauces, for anyone
who gives a fuck –
so he's marked the store down

and the rest of the staff
are staring at you
and it's not fair because –
oh
wait a minute,
I think … yeah,
here it comes, here
comes the poetic finishing line:

at least the moth got to spread its wings before dying here.

yeah
that'll do,
won't it? it'll have to.

WOMEN'S FIB AND OTHERS

watched
an old woman
yell at another
old woman

it was in a shop:
one of them worked there, the other didn't.

the old woman customer
was yelling at
the old woman worker,
jabbing her shoulder with her claw
and calling her stupid,
and despite them having similar genitals
and being of the same generation,
a set of genitals and age
apparently marginalised
in this society,
no one jumped in.

no gender
no age
no skin colour
no religion
and certainly no social class
can stop the prejudice
that a "HAPPY TO HELP" badge
inspires

you can be as
black and gay and poor and female
as the next black gay poor female
but if you have to wear that name badge
to bring in your taxable minimum wage,
then you are automatically a bully
and the other one
is the customer
and therefore your victim
and no amount of superficial similarities

will save you
from the victim's wrath

it's the only discrimination left
that isn't positive;
it's not positive,
this discrimination
for anyone can put on that badge
anyone at all
and it doesn't matter
for once
none of those things matter

and all anyone will see
is the badge:
you will be targeted
in some act of imagined revenge,
for sure,
but it's because of the badge
not all that other stuff

it's almost equality

so smile,
as the angry old woman approaches,
smile
and be grateful
for the absence of prejudice
as her claw
reaches for you …

COLLECTIVE WHAT

When a customer
has been yelling at you for quite some time,
holding up the queue,
and another customer leaves the queue,
comes over
and demands to know what's taking so long,
and they stand
side by side
ignoring each other,
both yelling at you, yelling over one another
like neither one exists?
well,
it doesn't leave you with much faith
in groups:
witch hunting is still our favourite pastime
and the fact that both of those customers
can walk away
certain
that they were the real victims
makes you
downright misanthropic
in precaution:
the witch burners were scared too.

LABELS LIKE BUMPER CARS

it was mental,
every customer cunt in town
had decided to shop at the same time

but every till was open
and every worker was serving,
so we were doing all we could
and we did it
for hours and
hours, hours
of faces, faces
haggling and complaining and insulting and assaulting
but we kept on, gotta pay the tax man somehow, eh? ha ha
we said as we scanned and packed and fought them off
and needed the toilet and food, but
we kept on

and I was fine, honestly
I didn't rise to any bait,
even when those meatheads threatened me
I just smiled and nodded with an empty stomach and a full
bladder
and served the next cunt
it
was
fine
ok

but then, fucking hell, then,
when someone on the afternoon shift showed up
and stood behind a worker, waiting to take over
so we could get our lunch breaks started,
this particularly jowly queueing customer cunt in my queue,
she goes: OH, I BET THIS NEW ONE'S JUST
REPLACING ONE OF THE OTHERS!
and shook her fat jowly customer cunt head,
well,
that got to me, ok, that got to me,
and it should get to you too, I mean

it was still the same amount of people serving, every till would
still be open,
it wouldn't make any difference
to how long she'd have to wait
but the idea that a shop worker would get a break, THAT
offended her? no, I thought, fuck
no, I'm not living in a world like this anymore,
and
when she was the second to next customer cunt in my queue
I said to my current customer cunt:
WELL, I'VE JUST SERVED YOU, BUT NOW I BET
I HAVE TO SERVE THE NEXT CUNT CUSTOMER
and it would have been seen as was it was: a really valid point
if it wasn't for the c-word
but she *was* a customer, dammit, a complete and total one
and you get my point, don't you? that
working starved with bladder cramp,
being that most subservient member of society,
it only encourages more prejudice,
like, say, taking away your breaks for no reason?
the point that
weakness invites aggression?
but if I'm so weak
why did the fat jowly customer cunt
nearly have a heart attack
where she had no heart?

send your answers to my store manager
like every other customer cunt.

I'M LOWER THAN A NONCE IN THE FOODCHAIN

been in the paper, him

he came in our shop
wearing a boxy suit,
jacket and trousers a different shade of black
and stained

he was at the courts today
it was in the paper
and he came the counter with a tinny of coke
and I had to serve him,
his fingers dripped
the little worn coin
into mine

he was in the paper again, him
he was in court
hence the boxy stained two halves of a suit,

they gave him 10 years

(which is double the age of the kids)

and just hours before
I'd said please
to him
and touched
those fingers
and fucking thanked him

keep the change, he'd said to me
with a small wet mouth

oh
I was changed
all right
and I've kept it with me
all right
oh.

WE BURN

sure,
when the fire alarm goes off
all the customers just stand there,
refusing to move

but when I threaten
to set fire
to one little brat
who knocked over my bean tin pyramid

suddenly everyone fears the flame?

selective standards, mate.

DRIVEN

fat bitch's mobility scooter broke down
right in the middle of aisle 8
and she started shrieking at me
to push her out of the store,
and I don't know what weighed more:
her, or the electric tank she was melted into,
but I'm telling you
their combined weight was nothing to sniff at,
and I don't know who was sweating more:
me or her
but I'm telling you
pushing a mould sodden walrus on wheels
transfers a lot of sweat
as well as generating a fair amount
of your own,
I actually slid off with a comic sound effect *squeak!*
a fair few times,
such a wet mass were we,
and at one point
I was clawing into the rock face of her bingo wings
for purchase
as her chins led the way
by pointing their beards
at the exit

and you might be wondering
how I can be so disrespectful
to someone differently abled?
well, the pain in my legs and arms
suggests I might be disabled now too,
and since she spent the whole time
she was inflicting
these disabilities on me
telling me to
HURRY UP,
why don't you ask her?

ho hum,
at least I can park closer to work now.

NEVER SURPRISED, ALWAYS AFFECTED

on boxing day
they moan
that there's not enough sizes
left on the sale rail,
they moan a lot
but then they buy it anyway
knowing it won't fit
knowing they'll bring it back tomorrow

and *you* know
you'll have to argue with them again
because there's no refunds on sale items:
you're 2 steps ahead

you know,
like how you spent Christmas Day
thinking about Boxing Day's arguments?
yeah,
that's how you spent your 1 guaranteed day off of the year:
drinking and fretting
over the aggro to come
because you're 2 steps ahead

you're powerless against your power,
having to watch it unfold
like a chess master
watching children play noughts and crosses,
and as with children
you are not allowed to kneecap the shits
even though you're trying to save them
from wasting
their 1 and only life
and yours:

you're always 2 steps ahead
3 days in advance
in your 1 and only life
and there's nothing you can do
to stop it

...
do customers know
they're going to die too,
or are they all
as eternal
as they act?

THE (A) INTERVIEW

he shakes your hand
and you sit down
and before either of you can start
exchanging lies and catchphrases
you see it:

world's best dad!
it says on a coffee stained mug

and all you can think is:
really?
if he had any decency he wouldn't have spawned them at all,
how are his children supposed to be grateful to a father
who drags them into a world
where he climbs the same ladders
that have been climbed for centuries
to no avail
and expects them to do the same
like it'll make a difference,
like next time will be better,
like things will change any day now
as opposed to
just
more,
much much
more
of the
fucking same?
do you really want to put your livelihood in the hands of such a
deluded puppet?
this breeder of puppets?
and what about you?
if you lie well enough here
he might hire you,
ask you to join him in this charade
passing time
in the most thankless way possible
until death
and you'll be complicit,

you'll be reinforcing the lie
to his precious puppet brats!
can you live with that on your conscience?

and sure enough
the claustrophobic cloud of futility
swells like black cotton
until the room,
his shitty little room of half-authority, it chokes and blurs
and you have to excuse yourself
before you say or do
something
you or he will regret

and he probably hates you now
but you just pity him
because pity lets you pretend
you're any better off.

COMMEMORATING MY 1000TH COMPLAINT

you ever look back
on how many customers you've offended,
how many days
and lives
you've supposedly ruined
with your "bad customer service"
and thought
wow,
I must be
the most evil,
most powerful
being
that ever lived,
so why
am I
still working here?

THE SUPERIOR EDUCATION OF THE UNEDUCATED

we shopworkers, we see you
at your most panicked,
your most stressed
your most vicious
and bored and lonely
we know who you really are
we know you are unhappy
and we don't like it any more than you do:
you think we want this knowledge?
our whole reason for being here
is that we're uneducated!
so why should we carry the burden
of knowing you
better than you know yourselves?
at least teach me something else
besides what a busy, ripped off, hard done to
victim you are …
or is that the lesson?
that I, the uneducated shop worker
am somehow better off
than you?
if so,
you must be as fucked as you pretend to be.

O(ri)FFICE

you haven't said anything in a while

so one of them asks you
THAT
dreaded question:

"what do you do?"

you tell them
and they look away

they go red
they blurt stuff out
in a panic
to change the subject,
they steal glances at you,
you're kind of like a car crash:
they don't want you
to see them
looking at you

and when your eyes meet
they go redder
and look away
and talk more
and look
and look away
and talk more …

the waitress comes over,
thank god,
you tell her you'll have tap water
and more breadsticks please

and the silence, jesus …

they are not bad people
but they work in an office

and can afford to eat here

and it's like
you're all in a fight
none of you
are interested in,
you know?

do you?

you all live in
post-80's Britain
post-millennium Britain
post-everything Britain

apparently
everyone
is broke and fucked

and yet
YOU are the only one
in this fancy place
who smokes
and needs to go to AA

YOU are the only one
who thinks this place is "fancy"

and
oh god
look at the menu,
what's those numbers
next to the word "water"
do they charge for water here?

of course they do you idiot,
everywhere else does
and like everywhere else
you're already in debt.

CONTACT

they either hover within earshot,
lamenting

"oh, where can the crisps be?
if only someone could tell me
where the crisps are …"

or

they march right up to you
and spit

"CRISPS?"

in your face,
like you're already enemies,
like you've been at war for years …

people still don't know
how to communicate

they still freak out
when faced with
their own species,

overcompensating
or exaggerating

to the point
where I have to
take a swing at them
or
run away.

THE PROTESTOR

DON'T YOU DARE!
she screams
GET YOUR FILTHY HANDS OFF ME, PIGS!

and the security guards
being male
have to back off

she's allowed to strut out of the shop
untouched

unlike the floor,
caked in all the fruit she'd thrown down
and stomped on
in protest of pesticides or farmers or something,
leaving her confident footprints
in the wasted lumpy wines
jellifying there …

quite how me doing overtime
mopping up her mess
makes the earth a better place
I don't know

but she has green hair
and wears an "F-Trump" t-shirt
so she's obviously more switched on than I –

I'm assuming the Trump she wants to "F" so badly
must have been thwarted,
otherwise why would she be here,
ruining my day?
it would be a case of literal
low-hanging fruit, would it not?
unless my free time
is more of a threat to her,
to the whole world,
than an unfucked Trump?

should an even more righteous customer
finally rid the earth of me,
I'm sure she'll be straight on the next plane
to the White House
to give Trump
the fucking he deserves

unless of course
she's spent all her benefit money
on green hair dye
and protest t-shirts,
useful social stalwart that she is

compared to me at least,
cordoning off the fruit aisle
with wet floor signs
as the customers swarm,
complaining.

GAS ATTACK

the automatic doors rattle apart …

a guy throws a bin bag
onto the shop floor
and walks back out.

the automatic doors rattle together again …

my supervisor starts shrieking the word "bomb"
and suddenly everyone's climbing over each other,
customers swiping vodka and crisps and declaring,
with not a little joy, that this is "the end"
as staff kick them towards the fire exit …

the guy, he had a McDonald's gherkin slice
stuck to one of his bare feet:
I doubt he could make the tea,
let alone a bomb
so I go over, open the bin bag:

my eyes boil in my head,
my skin flares,
I fall over choking …

it was his washing.

A SLIGHTLY BETTER CLASS OF SLAVE

my fellow shopworkers
I know how it is
I've been there
I am there
and I'll be there tomorrow
on the shop floor

of course
you get scared
of course you have IBS
of course you get depressed
and have panic attacks,
panting and shaking
as the row of faces looms
wondering when
the next insult
the next threat
the next attack
will come

you are right
to feel this way

if you didn't
if you could handle it
all the time
why, you'd have to be
a sociopath or a robot

you'd be like them:
those slaves to misery

you're a slave
but you're a slightly better class
of slave
the fact
that you get
frightened and depressed
means you know

this societal set up
is wrong

while they just reinforce
a capitalist hierarchy
they claim to be
victims of

of course
you've given up
on politics
on your fellow man

but
your weakness
is your strength,
for your panic
and sadness
your loss of faith

is rebellion,
is you
refusing to join
the collective misanthropy

you're a misanthrope
but you're a slightly better class
of misanthrope:

you've been forced into
disappointment
with your species
while they just look for opportunities
to be disappointed
in you,
you
are their opportunity
to be disappointed –
that's what's wrong
with society,

not you

your reaction
is totally understandable
your reaction
your rage, sadness and fear
your misanthropy,
it's all justified

even at your most
enraged
and futile
you're the best person
on the shop floor

and from one
scared
tired
politically bereft
misanthrope
to another:

I love you and I'm sorry.

www.ingramcontent.com/pod-product-compliance
Lightning Source LLC
Chambersburg PA
CBHW071701040426
42446CB00011B/1858